MISTY TWISTY KNOT

Understanding Emotions and Behaviors Associated with Anxiety

By Stephanie Brinkley Wellon

Illustrations by Katya Bowser

Misty Twisty Knot: Understanding Emotions and Behaviors Associated
with Anxiety

Copyright © 2014 by Stephanie Brinkley Wellon

ISBN-13: 979-8-9865891-6-9

Library of Congress Catalog Control Number 2014949258

Children's Fiction / Fiction
Printed in the United States of America

Dedication

*Identifying and understanding emotions and
behaviors associated with anxiety*

This book is written for all of us who have experienced feelings
of fear, worry, and nervousness on the inside as a result of
something we have seen, heard, or experienced.

For the little girl or little boy who feels or has felt scared, finds it
hard to sleep at night, and wants to experience a sense of
calmness and peace on the inside, you have been in my heart
and on my mind.

To the fear and worry that often takes root in our early
beginnings of childhood and paralyzes us thereafter: We come
now to serve you notice that you are no longer welcome to live
inside us anymore. "You must leave now."

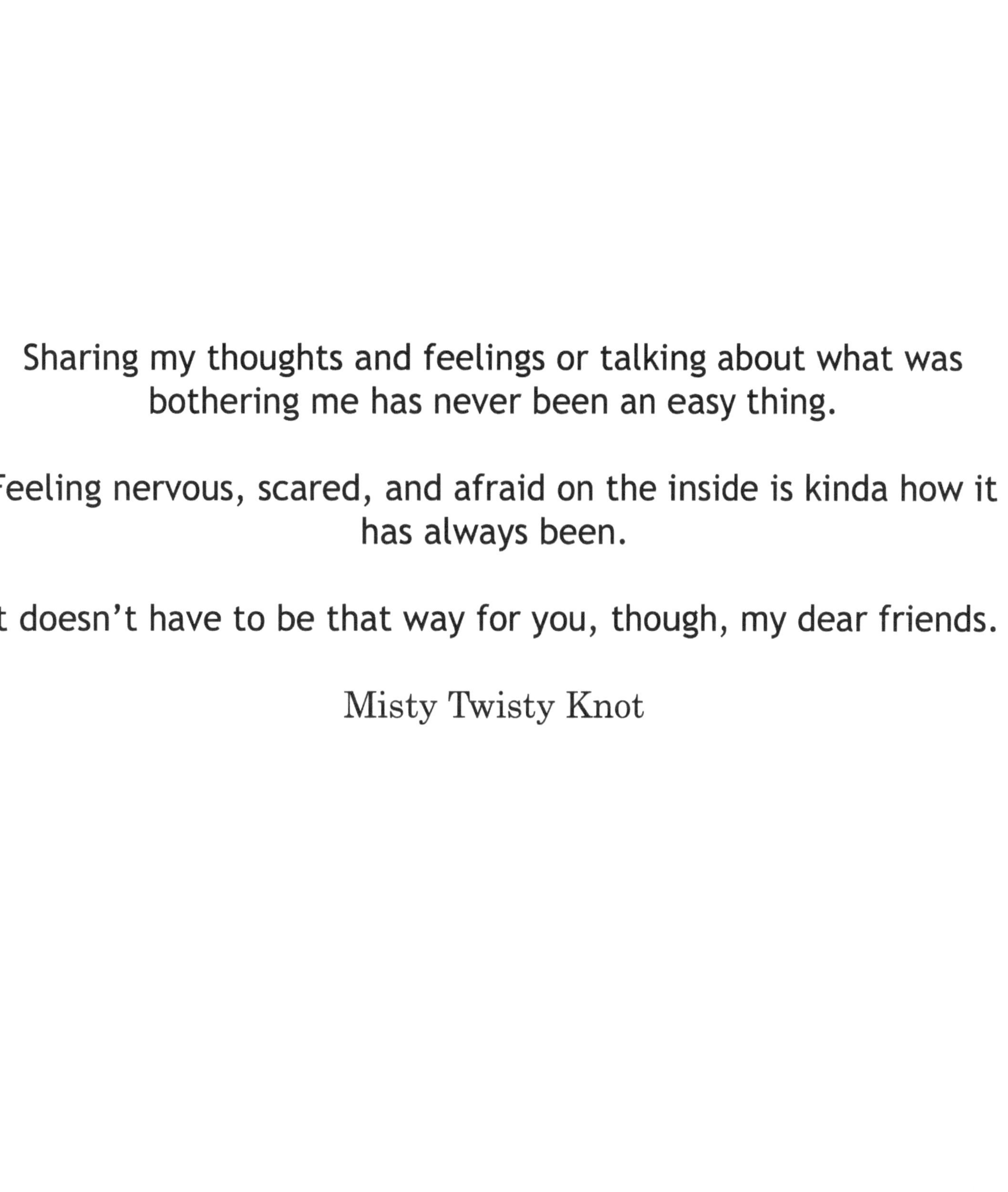

Sharing my thoughts and feelings or talking about what was bothering me has never been an easy thing.

Feeling nervous, scared, and afraid on the inside is kinda how it has always been.

It doesn't have to be that way for you, though, my dear friends.

Misty Twisty Knot

Hello! My name is Misty Mystique, but most folks call me Misty Twisty Knot.

They say I have *Ang-zi-e'-tee* (anxiety) because I worry a lot.

I worry all day, every day, about any and everything. I twirl my hair, bite my nails, and shake my legs.

And when I'm in class, because I'm not paying attention, my teacher yells, "Hey, Misty! Are you there?"

I count numbers and objects on the floor, and on the walls. And I think about things a million times until I am able to relax and move on.

I count in the morning, afternoon, and at night.
I find it hard to stop.

And...that's just not right.

And if I'm trying to read and finish a book, no matter how large, thick, or small, because I'm counting, I never get to finish. But guess what? That's not all!

I'm always on the go! Busy, busy, busy!
Hey, guys, that's just me. Sometimes my mind is
racing so much, I even forget to eat.

I can't focus or even concentrate:

And because I keep doing things over and over
again, I'm always late!

At night I constantly check the doors to see if they are locked. By the time I'm done, there's nothing left of me. When I sit down, I just go flop!

My hair is frizzy and frazzled because I twist it a lot. I guess that's where I got the name Misty Twisty Knot. I'm always tangled up tight just like a knot or like a twisted twig from a tree. And when it gets really bad, WOW! I can't even breathe.

I always feel wound up tight and on edge.
That's when I get away and hide under the
covers in bed.

I'd rather be alone. Sometimes I just don't care.
I'm exhausted all the time. This is just not fair!

My doctor says there's no reason for my tiredness. He says this is all in my mind. But when I'm alone, all I do is think, think, think! Geez! All of the time!

I can't sleep at night. I toss and I turn.
I have very bad dreams about scary monsters
that always do return.

Sometimes it's hard to breathe, and I feel tightness around my neck. My heart beats really fast and feels like it's about to jump right out of my chest!

Sometimes my head hurts, my tummy aches, and I don't feel my best. Sometimes I don't eat at all. I look at my food just sitting there.

I told my mom, my dad, and my best friend Andy a little bit of what bothers me. They said, "Everything will be okay." But I find that hard to believe.

Mom asked me again if something serious was going on. I responded, "Mom! Please just stop worrying and come on."

So she said, "Surely, my dear. But it must be something, for a lot has changed. We will get to the bottom of this, my dear, in just a few days."

"You've missed 31 days of school this year!" Mom exclaimed. "If we don't get to the bottom of this, I will go insane!"

Finally some help! Mom and Dad took me to this special lady that they know. I can't remember her name. That happens a lot. You see, I'm so forgetful.

I told her my name and that it was Misty Mystique, or "Misty Twisty Knot." I said that most of the time, I felt as if I were tied up in a knot.

She asked me to describe my fears and what
was bothering me.

We talked about my crooked thoughts and the
other yucky things that were way, way down
deep. Because they still frightened me.

It took me a while, but eventually I told her all of them. I cried, we laughed, and she taught me the most beautiful things in the end.

She said to me, "Misty Twisty Knot,
you know all of this is unfortunate and such a
shame. For you were born Misty Mystique.

And that's just a better name."

We blew bubbles, and that helped me to relax
while learning how to breathe:
"Take a deep breath in through your nose with
your mouth closed, hold for the count of 1,
exhale slowly, and then be at ease."

Finally learning how to relax was something
strange and new to me.

We talked about what I was thinking to see if my thoughts were crooked or straight. I learned that many of them were crooked and that I had to learn to think the right way.

I learned that what and how I thought had a lot to do with how I felt and behaved. I learned how to question my thoughts by asking, "Are you True or False" Or by saying, "Is there really any proof to you anyway?"

What helped me the most was learning that I needed to tell myself the truth. Yes! No longer hiding anything from me had become the right thing to do.

I told myself the truth about any and everything that was bothering me. Doing so made it much easier for me to tell the truth to Mommy, Daddy, Andy and me.

I learned to talk about my thoughts and feelings openly and honestly. I learned that writing my thoughts and feelings down by journaling was the most incredible thing.

I even named a few trusted adults that I could talk to about my feelings and thoughts!

Yes, there was Mommy, Daddy, my best friend, Andy, but there was also my teacher and my grandma and granddaddy.

Finally, I began to talk about my past and some of the things that had been so bad for me. Those things I had stuffed on the inside that made me just want to scream.

Now I'm not done yet dealing with this anxiety thing, and I know that many of us kids have it and that it can be really mean.

But take it from me, Misty Twisty Knot: if you want to feel better, first work on untying yourself from feeling like a twisted knot.

I did, and it's the most incredible thing!

Questions For My Friends

Can you think of any ways to help me unwind so that I can untie this knot inside of me and feel free?

Tell me some ways that you are just like me.

Has anyone ever talked to you about managing your "Ang-zi-etee?"